Blue, Candled in January Sun

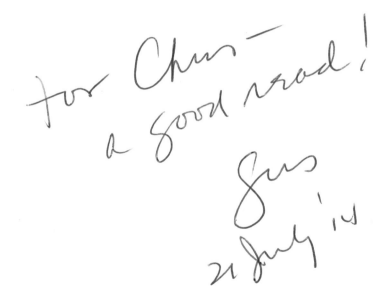

For Chris —
a good read!

Gus
21 July '14

Other Books by Sybil Pittman Estess

Elizabeth Bishop and Her Art, co-edited with Lloyd Schwartz, University of Michigan Press, 1983.

Seeing the Desert Green (poems), Latitudes Press, 1987.

In a Field of Words, co-authored with Janet McCann, Prentice-Hall, 2003.

Blue, Candled in January Sun

Poems by Sybil Pittman Estess

Cherry Grove Collections

Published by Cherry Grove Collections
P.O. Box 541106
Cincinnati, OH 45254-1106

Typeset in Aldine by WordTech Communications LLC,
Cincinnati, OH

ISBN: 1933456035
LCCN: 2005931940

Poetry Editor: Kevin Walzer
Business Editor: Lori Jareo

Visit us on the web at www.cherry-grove.com

For my son—Benjamin Barrett Pittman Estess

I would like to thank several other poets, Cyrus Cassells, Jill Alexander Essbaum, David Dodd Lee, Larry D. Thomas, and members of my poetry group, especially Laura Guidry and Kelly Patton, for their gracious suggestions and assistance with this book.

Grateful acknowledgment to the following publications for permission to reprint the poems noted, some in other forms or with different titles:

Adobe	"Daughter Can You Hear Me?"
America	"Memory"
Borderlands	"What the Citizens Need"
Brigid's Place Journal	"The Massacre at the Mosque"
Concho River Review	"Students Reading Together on a Bed"
i.e.	"Shrimp Fleet at Dawn"
Manorborn	"Trips With Her Dad"
Mellon Poetry Anthology	"Rothko Chapel in Black and White"
Midwest Quarterly	"The Rattlesnake Dream"
Mississippi Review	"The Anointment"
The New Republic	"Pretending You Were Joseph"
	"Undemonstrative"
New Texas	"Café Hacienda in Houston"
	"Coffee in Cazenovia"
	"There Are No Tigers"
The Odd Angles of Heaven	"Catechumen at the Blue Pool"
The Paris Review	"Blowing Sand May Exist"
	"Esther Decides"
	"One Thing It Was"
RATTLE	"In Passing"
SHADE VI	"View of the Twin Towers"
	"Scars"
Texas Poetry Calendar	"Bluebonnet Time"

The Texas Review	"Every Sorrow Can Be Borne"
	"Festina Lente"
	"Library Sestina"
	"Search for Perfect Blue"
	"Texas Memorial"
	"The Wide Net"
Western Humanities Review	"Keyboards"
	"Native on Land"
Windhover	"Ash Wednesday and the Houston Anglican Priest"
	"The Icon Room at the Villa de Matel"
	"Prayer for Her Hands"

Contents

I. Wait for the Wind

Pretending You Were Joseph

for Sue Collier Daniel, 1941-2005

You could consider your seven fat losses.
You could ponder the long lean years left.

You could count the rest of your exiled life
not double-crossed but an Egyptian-style feast

to be ceremoniously eaten. Too soon past.
You could discover that in any parched season

siblings, nearly forgotten and foreign, might knock
for the food of forgiveness. You could ask:

"In a famine of mercy must everyone fast?"

The Anointment

"Who anointed you?"
psychology books say. "Who
bestowed on you power to do

what you do?" Was it father,
mother, brother, aunt, friend?
Who planted the idea in your head

for you to be you rather than not?
Whoever said it, you are fulfilling
his or her dream. Perhaps anointing

came late—a scout leader, teacher,
another student who took vows with you
to become, someday, a painter or poet.

Maybe a bum you met at a crossroads,
who said something significant.
A builder of houses who chuckled,

"You nail those nails very well!"
You grew into a house constructor.
Or your mom said your cookies seemed

tasty. You beamed, took up cooking
full-time. Now it's today, closer
to the end of life. Have you ever

once chosen the one you yourself would
choose for your anointment? Which model
would you follow past middle age? Please

remember. Develop a moving screen
of your history, your life. Survey
the whole scene of persons you have

known. Perhaps by sixty, you could
create a new ceremony. Maybe Christ
could do it. Buddha, Mohammed. Imagine

it: the anointer might be yourself. You
could pour the oil into your hands. Then
lift it to your head, allow sticky liquid to run

down your face until the decision blinds
your eyes awhile. You could say to yourself,
"I cherish you, whatever

it is you have chosen. The way you
have decided or had, by necessity,
to choose. Now, here, whatever

it is you happen to be or do,
I call you out.
I bless *you*."

"Blowing Sand May Exist"

Highway sign near Clovis, New Mexico

All she knew was that grit got in her eye.
Her husband, who was driving, thought
it had been written by a frustrated philosopher.

He came straight home and wrote an essay—
forty pages—on all its possible meanings.
She had been meditating as they whizzed by.

She didn't even see it. "If it may exist,"
he reasoned, "it also may not."
We were out on the desert, like life.

We were out where we all need reminders
and signs. And after reading them we think
of heeding. Warned, we wait for the wind.

One Thing It Was

Of course it was animus projection
or neurosis. It was her search for God.
Her Dionysian-lack. A yen to frequent
artists, a weakness for Italian males.

Perhaps just a failure to pray?
Call it *recherché du temps perdu*
(they were fifty). It was her Dickinsonian
quest for spiritual bliss, a fatal infatuation.

It was her old trick of giving-in-order-
to-receive. Both of their failed bondings
at homes. Unfaithfulness, and guilt, and sin.
Unliberated leanings on the wrong men.

 Fascination with fire and butterflies.
But then, after all labeling, fashionable
name-calling, blaming, nit-picking second
guesses, some simple, quite out-moded facts

 remain: *one thing it was was love.*

Esther Decides

She was only a woman, and no more
than his latest wife who was commanded
not to come before him without the grant

he gave away, candy to children.
Although she was beautiful, she had an
inner life she had harrowed a long time.

Often she danced with her soul mates, or she
meditated. Sometimes she prayed. Sometimes
she went to see her shrink. She paid the bills

herself and knew her animus. (Haunted
by the ghost of her lost father, she thought
she slew it every year on his death day,

begged him not to bother her much more.)
But when her cousin called her to act
for her people, for Yahweh, and for herself,

she weighed it on the gauge, as Mary did
one distant day. Then Esther took Spirit,
pumped her lungs with it, breathed seven breaths.

So she walked straight ahead, content to be
a Jew at risk, with good breasts. She wanted
no heaven. She faced him, female to male.

He looked. He decided. But both could live
with themselves a long time after what they said.
Esther alone had caused them to choose. (Now

she tells her dead dad all this as they talk.)

Students Reading Together
on a Bed

One black. One white. They lie on her bright-white
bed right next to the teacher's room in the boarding

house where the owner has a rule that two persons
of the opposite sex may not close the door.

One is fat, one thin—they've been good friends,
she says, since high school. It must be a short

story: freshman English text. The teacher overhears
the soft words chanted aloud. Sounds like O'Connor:

". . . and he badly needed redemption. . . ."
Something like that. Then, "He knew he wouldn't

find it in church." They, of course, are not
in church. They are not in the living room,

either—or even just on her light bed. They float
in the kernel of hot eros—only she doesn't know it.

The girl thinks she is helping him learn. She thinks
it is only an innocent land. She doesn't sense

the many minefields of touching—if not his
clothed genitals or his skin. The listener thinks

this is what beds for two are always about:
hunting for someone's hidden half—the unearthed,

not easily scraped. Hoping treasures are there
to take. Being drawn like a miner to what

(for lack of better words) we call the finer minerals
of (if not his or her body) someone's blue heart.

"You Start With One Thing

and end up with another and nothing's
like it used to be, not even the future."★

Like the baby as it dares to coo, crawl, walk.
Like any marriage maturing down scarier slopes.

That hope you picked up by mistake moved
your mind somewhere different from your plan.

The blue suit of yours still hanging
in the closet may not change, yet its thrifty

uses can. What habits do we lend each
other, dear, with years? Caring lovers,

partners, friends, purposes that stood us in good
stead may some day go—though we surely

never knew it so before last Lent, last year,
earlier. Do love's beauties sear and die

with time? Or need from yesterday appear as today's
joy? See far into tomorrow's begging spaces,

empty, willing and waiting to be fed and filled.

★Rita Dove, "Corduroy Road"

Keyboards

Early each morning she writes to him from
Georgia. From Vermont, he answers her by noon.
At cocktail time they want to exchange some

onions, olives, or cherries. But quite soon
their clocks tick to powder, pajamas, sheets.
She teaches sociology. He moon-

lights after his day in math. All she meets
on her graphs and charts, everything he finds
in his figures say their years and feats

are likely not to last. What binds
them may be such facts. They met by accident
at Narragansett Bay: a meeting of like minds

that is rare. Both bodies, too, seem hell-bent
on dancing through two evenings in Memphis,
then Mississippi. They'll have the luggage sent:

over a hundred combined falls with that kiss
from some other past not quite forgotten
yet. Days, they ask the keyboard what love is—

is it laughable at their age—this skin
with goose bumps? Then they wonder, "What will
our several children say?" What kind of sin

can all this cause? Who will pay the bill
or where would they live? How to keep their
current careers? Just as crucial, will

he burn her toast, break her heart? Would she dare
to tell him how to clean the sink? How long
would they have if they began now? (Her hair

is graying.) They have no answers—right or wrong.
It is like asking if the two would critique
each other's prose—or if death would bring song

or pose problems. At dawn each one will reek
of their state. They'll fetch slippers, wonder where
their glasses are. Then they'll brush bridges sleek

with Close-Up. While quiet, down here,
a machine longs to tell them what they seek:
silent, somewhere, someone can surely care.

Undemonstrative

I was living happily in Boston when he called:
"Will you fly on a crow's back back to Houston?"

"I don't love you—romantically," I replied.
(I am not pretty and do not speak well.)

"No matter," he argued. "That will come."
I returned, and we had a lovely courtship, then

wedding. When people ask me, "Do you love
him?" I am honest. I say, "No, but he is

the best of good husbands so I can't complain."
Forty years together and I never loved

my first husband either. My background, I suppose.
It's my background: undemonstrative.

I don't remember my mother kissing
or hugging my brother, my sister, or me.

She was sort of . . . Victorian. But my sister
and I were close anyway. Since I married

her husband, I moved into her old house,
wear her old clothes he never removed.

Last week was her birthday. I saw myself

buried with her, felt her in my bones. But I,

who don't know about feelings, am content.
It hardly matters at all.

Coffee in Cazenovia

She sips coffee in Cazenovia
from a gold-daisied, Syracuse China cup.

She asks herself, What makes the soul grip?
Does it stick by *taste*? This thickly brewed bean—

the hot, sweet caffeine steaming. Or by *smell*?
Sniffs of French wine, mint tea, brie, roses, oil?

Later, that lake gleams in mid-August light. Those boats
bask in late summer's ease. Are loves bound tight

by *sound*, she considers? His silence. The gift of one
voice from her childhood? Their own boy baby's cry

that long night? Does *touch* determine the Spirit?
Yours, ours, theirs, its, God's, pain's. Everything

in our *sight* kisses, then shifts, she knows.
Then these so dearly missed—after death.

Native on Land

When we descend from the Grand Canyon
on the cold eastern side, Highway 64,
toward the Little Colorado Gorge,

we come upon the vast Northeastern
Arizona flats named "Painted Desert"—
huge and barren, unspeakable

multi-colored space. Near the corners
before the road runs out, we go east
out across the freezing, poor reservation.

We stop at the roadside market
in zero weather: December 26.
Here Indian mothers and children,

grandmothers, grandchildren sell jewelry
as always. They have waited for hours
camping in old cars with heaters, hoping

some winter tourists will buy. At four
o'clock, I hand an old woman a twenty
and she fumbles for a five. Bracelet

on my arm, we take the road to Flagstaff,
a warm house off Country Club Drive. Before
we reach Wupatki monument and volcanic

Sunset Crater, to the right of our car
in the clear, mauve desert pre-sunset, white
San Francisco peaks appear. On the shoulder,

two young Navajo men stride. Their legs,
miles high, climb the sky. Their long, thick hair
shines black. I see it blowing, strong as the wind.

II. Close to Her Home

Rothko Chapel in Black and White

So you sit here in the black seeing the ambiguity
of pretending anything is black and white, just
that: you see it, or do not. You like him or love her
or you don't—and she you. You either remember
her or you won't. You've been here for an hour
looking at the black on white, hearing all the silence.
You have seen it from fourteen ways, at least. All
the colors hung on these hued walls. What you need
is someone to tell you what it really means:
this black, white, nothing. How it's as easy as that.

Café Hacienda in Houston

It is so hot here in July she has
to imagine she is somewhere else,
will survive: old Marrakesh, maybe,

or Mexico. So at 10:00 o'clock, just after
her class, she heads to Café Hacienda
to sit in hot shade, drink iced coffee,

eat fajítas with guacamole, pico de
gallo, cilantro, jalapeño as well. *Mucha
gente* are just awake here on Canal Street:

Latinos, Gringos, and she here in pink
adobe. The loud music sings and traffic—
buses, trucks, old cars—makes too much

noise. The proud beats twang on that jukebox.
For four bucks she goes far, becomes nearly
lost somewhere close to her own house

but conceptions away. She thinks that one lives
where one lives—as we exist anywhere
(with a mate, a child or a friend)—a while in our old

mind-sets. Then one day, cold, something ends.
We happen, head-on, maybe by heat, to be
where they are—and meet *them*.

Shrimp Fleet at Dawn

It's Rosh Hashanah, but not to Vietnamese
shrimpers. Tet comes later. Shrimp boats
rest all night until dawn. Then diesel engines
rev. Lights on the tall spars blink like they are Stars
of David in a row going to cast out lucrative nets.
(Though this is far from Galilee.) Someday
one hurricane will level all this channel scene (the cafes,
fish markets, the Pattersons' fifty-year-old
beach house) to debris. But not yet.
So at seven o'clock, before she goes to teach
in a town not her city but near it, grackles
and gulls squawk, as the southeast glows
gold-pink. On the deck by the channel, Culex
mosquitoes bite, and a tiny bug-eyed frog is so lost
he must have sipped bourbon all night. She picks him up,
places him on grass. Ships inch toward the president's
war in Kuwait as fishermen speed toward the horizon
also. She sees the sun, six inches high,
singe Galveston Bay, like a flame.

Catechumen at the Blue Pool

Paddling toward Jane, at twilight, is an old
nun in her life jacket, bright blue. Jane is
quiet for the day at the Catholic retreat.

Here women believe things are possible,
especially the "impossible." They start
with exercise on summer evenings before

any dim night of the soul. The lady
says she is glad Jane has come for the day
to pray—although Jane is Protestant.

She assumes never again will there be
a convent as big as this one. For God,
she claims, is a spirit of change. Acres

here in the city are gardened, Eden-like.
Geraniums, hibiscus, fountains, grottos,
paths wind everywhere to statues

of the virgin. The nun says she thanks Christ
all the time for Vatican II, floating folks
such as her and Jane together. She works

with cancer patients, trusts that the Lord
never notices what denomination any
suffering woman is, or dying man.

She hastens to say that parents should not
wait for the church, but teach God themselves
to their own. She pants words between breaths,

while stroking. It is good, Jane muses, the nun
does not swim alone. At her age, a body-buoy—
blue as Mary's mantilla—brings

brilliant company. Near fifty, Jane tries
laps when her aged confidante leaves her
in indigo silence. Jane wills to believe.

Icon Room at the Villa de Matél

Worshipers focus, as few of us ever do,
on a hub from which to leave this place,

the icon room at the convent—Villa de Matel.
Each chair is full. Lighted candles fill space

with scent. Not the same strong incense burning
in the meditation room now during 4:30 vespers.

This is subtler. Still as statues, they stare
at those saints. "Something will emerge," the nun

had told Louise. She is that tiny sister who sits
with her back so straight. Louise looks at the image

of Mary, made in Russia. She's having trouble
with her son, who is eighteen, confused.

"Treat him as an icon of chaos," the sister had said.
"Notice your own." Jesus sits on Mary's

lap when he was near seven years old, the age both
church and Piaget claim we become

accountable. They are shrouded with auras of red,
and round halos, gold. Blue rings at their wrists.

Their arms wide, their palms open and up.
Louise stares as long as she can. Then she

leaves the people there, motionless, still—as if they
are insane on this trafficked, fast-speeding globe.

Pondering Iconography

Church of St. Francis, Waco, Texas

The only Anglo, she enters in tennis shoes.
The guitar music begins and the Holy Spirit

prepares to descend in Spanish. Murals
of fourteen stations of the cross haunt nave walls.

Frescoed on baldachino are a series of progressive
paintings: Franciscans with large gold crosses,

like albatross swords. They conquer savage
Apaches who try to wound kind missionaries—

with arrowheads and blows. But then, Indians
bow low to might and myth of cross and these

Christians. They go slowly through ritual until
Eucharist. She eats it though she is Episcopalian.

Rosaries remember Mary. Only one icon amid
white lighted candles is dark: the Virgin of San Juan.

Her black straight hair falls from her head to hips,
to feet. Her dress is light blue and white. The rest,

all the Christs in all stations—even the resurrected
one above the altar—are Anglo men the Hispanic

congregants wish for but never know:
patient, kind, less demanding. Their Jesus

is like snow, pallor white.

The Cemetery on the Hill Behind the College in Brenham

As she walks fast among the dead, their bones
under this secular ground, she sees new stones

are not like the old poured and pocked ones.
Her shoes also are not like theirs, weighing tons.

So they wouldn't walk, as she does, to exercise—
not far from her classes—a new enterprise

at lunchtime. Deities, too, are different
nowadays. Ancients lately have been rent

like the veil of the temple once: in two
directions—out, deep within. And the new

faith way is walking, keeping the body fit
by Reeboks. Body's cathedral of soul, but it

isn't like Solomon's, nor like Notre Dame.
It doesn't reach high or wide. No, far from

it. She goes in circles surrounding this graveyard,
staying in motion, keeping up, her bard

is body, not spirit. She is not like this stuck
angel in rock past people put here. (No, our muck

is not fiery but icy cold: old ozone layer
bleeding. Most families split. Bayer

aspirin making ulcers. Our hurting heads
in PC's, more e-mail than hearts can read

or sort.) Does meditation seem mysterious
waste? Do we know God? Would numinous

taste hot or brief or condensed enough for us,
an incensed though frozen generation? Thus

said a past prophet: "What does the Lord
require of you, oh [wo]man? To do good,

love mercy, walk humbly with God."
Now no other savior. Yet her real feel of sod.

Ash Wednesday and the
Houston Anglican Priest

He doesn't know what the lilies are named.
He has owned them for seventeen years,

tropical as the bananas here in Houston. Pinch
the green, slick lily-leaf off, put it in dirt, see

how it flourishes. A parishioner gave him
two bunches in 1977. "No trouble," he said.

"You can't kill them." They haven't succumbed
in all this time. He's had at least three hundred.

Denise Levertov, who came to read to his
church after she was converted, took two back

to Palo Alto one March to keep. "Do they bloom?"
she wondered. "No," he said. "A pity," the poet peeped.

So today—Ash Wednesday—he goes to water
one gangly bunch in his study, by windows, near

the view of high rises. They are dry, have grown
long, winter fronds, rising high toward the sky.

He should have trimmed them through cold.
Now, like kings' crowns, lily points creep

up toward the ceiling. Almost ugly. Yet
for this Lent, flowers are there! Tiny, white,

alpine. Delicate lily blooms prove him a liar.
"So like our lives," the priest thinks. We wait

and wait, even as Jacob tarried to marry sweet
Rachel. We almost cease imagining miracles.

Years loom, he knows. Suddenly, patience pays
in white bloom.

Blooms from Bogotá

Chameleons have nervous breakdowns here
in all this endless color: purple, pink, vermilion

on Fannin Street in Houston. Since she moved
here, Lara has loved fondling, consuming such

loveliness. Every season has its own
scent, color and shape, hue and variety.

But today, when her plane lands in Bogotá,
she sees plastic bubbles blistering earth.

Football-field-size hot-houses. Millions.
Her Fannin Street flowers multiply perfectly

grown with chemicals in Columbia. Sown near
airports for easy export. But Ana Gomez's

South American fingers, toes, have turned black
as any coal miner's lungs. Irene Gomalez

vomits for days when they spray right
in her face. Maria Lopez's child has only

half of its head. It's said: wells are poisoned.
Mirror-like streams are soiled as soil is,

chastity ripped. Women workers take
to their beds. So blooms must grow without

them picking soon—the roses, the mums,
the glads. Yet Lara's home city, Houston,

craves beauty and brilliance as ever, and buying.
Blind millions will still stop, be seized, and shop.

Sea's Brew

Fiercest wind she's ever felt here batters
her face. High seasweed-strewn waves

roar. Loudest she's known except in storms.
Days later she learns: this was already named

"Allison." It would flood devastated Houston
as antithesis of Holy Ghost's fire. That night,

she was aware only of senses, sounds like her
childhood. And gulls yelling. She was alone.

The man out in that twilight, bobbing, was her
Daddy fifty years ago, floating waves. It was

almost Father's Day. Her dad had been dead
nearly four decades, yet this scene—out six

glass panes, doors five floors high—comforted
her more than any sound in cities can. More

than the view, more than smelly memory, sea
sounds are her memory music. They're cresting,

spilling. Resting, filling her bones with scenes
and sounds of him—her father—teaching her

to love sea. It was Florida's Caribbean blue-green.
It was sugar-white sand, as it used to be there.

It was her dad following her here, all this
long, fatherless time. She heard his years,

back then, soothe her restlessness. Even
by that Texas-brown, brewing gulf. Sea once

more restoring her—as then. Splashing,
crashing, in loudest rhythm, again and again.

Bluebonnet Time

When the bluebonnets come out in Texas,
Lady Bird takes a walk around the ranch
near Austin. She is really too old anymore
to care for them, but she loves red paint-

brush covering Lyndon's grave. She recalls
her life with him. How he loved her re-name.
"Claudia" was never quite right for her soul.
But was he really right? Not always faithful,

he was often a boor, an ass. Her father
told her Lyndon might never forego low class.
Yet he knew her, saw deeper than she could
touch. For that she tolerated, no, adored him.

He leaned on her—even to make this place
as beautiful as their past lives. Now she has
planted rye grass—or had the hands plant it.
She sits a while at his grave, dressed in black.

Walking back, she shivers, without her coat.
Like Penelope, she wants no other lover, though
she can't see him now on the Pedernales.
Is he returning? Is she teasing herself?

Will she or will she not ever find him there
again? She would want to know this if she
could weave, unwind. The world is meditation,
as she believes. "Bird?" "Claudia?"

Her two names haunt and call. Pausing, she is
glad she scattered seed in their winter wind.

Blue Field

The day they sat down in someone's spring field
of bluebonnets in Texas last April was a Friday

near a town named "Roundtop." That dear day
was mostly like any other late in that month

that year. Yet they were there, where mostly
they are not. They were aware they were there,

mindful of flawless blue blooming by them.
Consummate friends smiled, posed the two

of them in the color: all blue as far as you cared
to hope or could see. Nothing else like this

crowning click could be in Texas this spring, like this
dearth of daily task. Then when the friends ate

late lunch at the Roundtop Cafe there where butter
was good but the waiter too fat, they were back

to their fact. They both checked their watches
that would not stop as they wished. But before,

they split fish with no conflict. Fried fresh, better
than they had hoped it would taste. Better, fairer

by far, their hour, day, way, a blue field.

III. Hands, Stay With Us

For Marion, 1921-2003★

★*The year of our mother's stroke, at Christmastime, paralyzed, Mother whispered to my sister, "I feel." "What do you feel?" my sister asked. "I feel blue," Mother replied.*

Trips with Their Dad

The family never knew where they were going.
Once he wrote to their mother inside a tiny
capsule and placed the note in a big box
under the Christmas tree: "Today you'll spend

the night beneath the bright lights of a big city."
They lived eighty or so miles north of one,
but as far away as Paris from Moses
or Job—psychological and cultural

continents away. Also, her Daddy hated
New Orleans. He disdained those French frills:
unnecessary accents were just pretense.
He would have despised crepes, had he tasted

them—or beignets. (He disliked all sweets.)
So he also thought quite foolish
the Polynesian food they picked Christmas
night by the loud airport near their motel.

Chuckling, he asked the Cajun waitress
if they cooked country cornbread, crowder peas.
But bright lights excited him: electric Santas,
angels and mangers. All the fifties were

full of these, and of those strange Catholics
of Louisiana. The huge houses and street cars

on St. Charles Street were unlike anything
anyone mostly from Mississippi had seen.

Once in the summer it was Daytona Beach
for two weeks—the longest family
holiday ever. The elder daughter's memories
are heavenly: block rooms, screens, breezes,

Atlantic waves she fought with him. (Her nine years
they had been fighting.) He hadn't told them
where they were going until they got there. At age
four, her sister got sick with a fever, believing

every mile to be a mere hoax. Older,
she always knew he meant what he said
when he intended to head out for somewhere.
When he died—at forty-seven—pain

had pounded him for four years. She knew
he meant business, too. The last he said was,
"I wrote your tuition check. Why did you come?"
Could she have claimed, "I know where

you are going?" Robbed him of his old game.
Was she to lie to him—say he was not really
dying? Despair trapped them. Let them travel
nowhere by surprises. They each knew they knew.

Prayer for Her Hands

After Mother's stroke. Fall, 2002

All their hands were beautiful, like Hopkins'
"dappled things." Before thirty-nine, when
cancer killed her, my mother's youngest

sister used to squeeze lemon juice on her hands.
She bleached out brown, her hands soft.
Both of her breasts fell, but she kept her hands.

I wonder if she still loved them. Even at sixty,
now, I do not suffer age spots, like my mother's,
whose hands lie stroke-stiff, immobile. I won't

rub them out, try to hide spots if they come.
Hands, separate from the womb I might
lose or my breasts. Mother's feeling, her

painter's work, she has lost. My mom's
hands and her sisters' were like mine: sturdy
hands that have worked, scrubbed often,

cooked, washed old pots and pans. Hands,
stay with us, even clenched, as mother's
paralyzed hands are. Brindled, broken,

to our long end.

Daughter, Can You Hear Me?

When I call my mother, usually it's about triglycerides,
church, sometimes scripture or prayer. Or her
neighbors, the flowers, freezes, cold air. But yesterday

she had been to her doctor and driven back by herself forty
miles. What we talked about was something urgent,
something she desperately wanted

to tell me, something she had not anyone else, not even her
husband, to tell. It was the sunset, she said, and the white
cloud she had seen—how huge it was,

and how strange. How she watched it for thirty-some miles.
Saw all the shapes it took, the pink glow it became.
How she had never seen anything like it,

and how she had thought of little else since. How
she had dreamed of it, how she thanked God. How
she had wanted me to see, exactly, that scene.

There Are No Tigers

"There are no tigers in the back yard. She is
lying," he said to her mother about her when
she was three. Her father, who had a hard time

with flowers, all things to be grown, including
kids. He had come up on a farm earlier.
How he hated grass, even—having to mow it.

But the green things he despised most were
wiles. Imagination fits in her even when
she was that tiny tot with lots of space,

endless energy to see those big beasts,
growling. She was proud, too, when he hit
her for fibbing or racing by his mowing

machine that never cut down her tiny
vow not to tell him more tales. Now
she's near sixty. Those stripe-filled faces

petition her to play. Like haunts, they follow
for fun. She watches well, does not tell him,
dead, all wild things he could let her see

or say.

Library Sestina

Mississippi, 1950: age 8

Her mother always let her take the bus
to heaven for a nickel. In town she waited
with innocent breath, wondering alone where
was the nearest stop to the paradise library.
She walked some six or seven blocks away—
then the ascent up the circular, stone steps.

The Hardy Boys connived up those sky-high steps.
And Nancy Drew solved crime where the dear bus
ferried her. The Bobsey Twins played far away
from her house. Seven days she had slowly waited
to meet them Saturday. That ivy-bricked library
was not like her bookless home. It was there where

Miss Librarian said "Shhhhh!" too loudly. (Nowhere
but here, she mused, could that lady live, so skinny!) Steps
raised her to creaky hardwood, the library—
floors glazed. Then green bindings boarded a bus
going slowly home with her. (Each week she waited
a Genesis-creation for giant tires taking her away.)

Every time she had to return to a plain life—away
from magic to her family—and also to where
most mysteries stayed unfixed, she still waited

to go once again to repose—up those steps
where she could see Susan B. Anthony (by bus).
Bound orange, Esther was also in the library.

And it was in the same old library
that she wrote MGM, mailed her letter away
to Hollywood and went back home by bus.
"You have made a movie of Moses, but where
is Esther's?" she composed. She had risen on steps
of stone to reach that protest. As she waited

patiently for a reply never arriving, she waited
turning new pages in the huge, high old library
still there (being renovated now)—those steps
still rising. Today, when she flees, goes far away
from her own flawed house, that library is where
she yearns to reach by her mind. No, by her bus!

But she's strayed. Oh, she's weighted, a long way away
from her lighted library with its bind. She lives where
she can't mount those steps. She finds it won't come—that bus.

Texas Memorial

Galveston. Fall, 2004, during U.S. Presidential campaign

An outside memorial to Vietnam dead
stands at Moody Gardens Park—by a fake
beach on the bay, created waves. Bordered
with green palms beside red hibiscus, bright
yellow, pink, purple, other huge tropical
flowers and jungle plants. Close by is their
Imax Theater showing spectacular shows,
the butterfly exhibit in the tall, pyramid
dome across from the happy resort hotel.

But here, in five rows, five to a row, stand
twenty-five gray-black granite pylons.
Three names on each. The monument's floor
is hard, pink, Texas marble. Its square
floor-base slants down, deep on one side.
The architect writes: downward means pain
and death, the worsening horror. All dates,
here, are quite clear. No debates.

What I remember most
of all the terrible ten years: I can't forget
August, 1965. They came to tell my future
stepfather and his wife, John's mother: their
one son was shot in his heart at Chu Lai
the first hour his unit stormed the beach.
John was exposed on the top of the tank—

a First Lieutenant Marine leader, age twenty-
two. ("I am two and twenty./ And, oh, 'tis
true. 'Tis true.") One thing I know is
his mother said she already knew when
they came. She told them Johnny's best gun
fell from his room's rack on the wall—
in the night—same time, same hour as there.
"He is dead," she had said.

What my mind can't erase is that I was
the last girl he was with on the mainland—
the night before he shipped out from New
Orleans to Honolulu. Margaritas, shrimp,
dancing in Biloxi. I listened to Johnny tell
his Marine career dreams. I heard later
how his mother died of cancer and grief.

I saw his dad marry a young widow, my
mother. We all lived twenty-five more
years with his father's bottled rage. What
we sensed was that the dad never could
sort out those days, his anger as blurred as
cataract sight. He had few ways to order
distortion. Medalled Colonel in Battle of the Bulge,
he stayed Democrat. Wounded. He and mother
roved to D.C. often to that dark monument wall,
slanting down from the beginning, near where
John's name is. They rubbed and rubbed on
John's name more than once. But John's body
could not come forth. Mother framed and hung
Johnny's portrait in their main room. We had

to see it, always, as we turned lights on or out.
The room's wall wore John's image, gold-
surrounded. But silent—as these black stones
here in Galveston—as all those plots of our own
fifty-thousand, now forty-year dead. Stopped
stepbrothers. (Not to speak of the living-
deceased. The mind-mangled. The maimed.) Seventy-
five men died from Galveston County. Their dates
are marked here, none even thirty years old. About
their deaths, death-days, battles they may or may not
have fought, here no dispute.

IV. As Much As You Consciously Could

Ordinarily

On wars: Kosovo

No real bonds between us. As my friends
and I talk at a conference about God,

somebody slits this baby's throat. Somebody
else takes its shoes, another its picture.

Still a fourth denies it. Then somebody
hacks off the old lady's right foot, the one

who lies left of her gray husband, shot.
Hardly anyone sees them rotting in woods.

What was it someone missed? Imagination?
Soul, sympathy or religion? I remember

the root: *Re-ligio:* to re-connect. I recall
what they say of the Reich: 1943. I re-think:

how no one did anything then too. I link
that to Hannah Arendt saying of Eichmann

what stunned her: he was ordinary folk,
she said, following ordinary orders

on a merely non-extraordinary day.

The Massacre at the Mosque

Tomb of the Patriarchs, Hebron, West Bank, Israel: 2/25/94

His gun shoots on the day that Kerrigan
Skates. His gun shoots when we have said
About peace "It is finished." His gun shoots
By one man, one mind. His gun shoots by a Jew,
An American. His gun shoots by a finger
On a hand, on a body, a masque, which says
He adheres to God. His gun shoots in an ancient
Place I have seen where Rachel, the mother of each
Race, is not interned, as they claim. She burned
In Ramah where scripture declares she wept
For her dead children. *She cried for her kids*
Because they were no more. They were no more
Because of war. Oh why have we not beat swords
Into hooks for pruning? Why had he not pruned
His hate? Why have we not heard Rachel wail?
In this state of our end, this endless century,
Since near sixty silenced surrounding one mosque
In Ramadan,

How shall we now, like her,
for them sing our sad, sad songs?

The Rattlesnake Dream

The dream you had about the six-foot rattler
springing up at you past your head. Image

came from the scene in Cather's *My Ántonia,*
the text you just taught. Luckily, you woke

before it bit—the fangs being on their way
down. It didn't destroy you—old black serpent

who took even Eve for her ride. Did it really
disappear when you woke? Where did it hide?

They say serpents can heal. See it as symbol.
It stood straight up on its legs. It had eyes,

an expression so terrible and maliciously human.
It would have struck you dead without your own

craftiness: you woke, spoke your mind to timeless
snake. Then you went about your actual day

carrying on your usual, good-evil way, choosing
the better one as much as you consciously could.

Most China Chips

Her mother was at her house for holidays.
Mother's home gone now, her mind, memory.
All bright photos will not summon, call
what mother shuts out or has had shut.

Mother gets sick, pneumonia, while daughter
tends her. Then out of the blue, daughter
is struck too. The husband has gone
to his old, moldy folks, shut in. The grown

son gets pissed off over some money mix-up.
Then she dreams of him—as a three-year-old
toddler who needs her nourishing him. (Who
feeds whom?) Questions of all fine china—

which she loves to eat from, look at, fondle,
especially on Christmas, each Epiphany. When
few things seen unlighted. Then new January:
plain same cycle to Lent. What use is Limoges,

yesterday, memories, flawless present, history?
Mostly we consume toast, tea, life from chipped,
everyday, too common cups. Containers from
which some sustain any serendipity and sole hope.

View of Twin Towers From Bleecker St.

In the Village

They tower to the south, out the window.
Two weeks we stay, amazed, on Bleecker.
NYU seems happy, close by below.

We come to culture that July. Fellow
Friends lend us four rooms. So, seekers,
We see stalagmites. South out our bedroom window:

Tall towers. Night lights. We're awestruck. Though
They're stable, they sway. Cowered, weaker,
NYU appears happy—to be close-by. Below.

We learn the Big Apple, we think. But we're still callow
As we trade high NYC for low house, Upstate. Peekers,
We peeked daily to the south. Out the window

Early, each day. Finally, to one tower's top. I bellow,
"I have to get down!" You snap rivers. Meeker
(like NYU), I am content on the ground. Close by.

We worry about fire. But by plane? Highest hell—oh
Who could choose it? Quick! Run! Down! Quicker!
They tower to the South in our minds. Out that window.
Like NYU, we are some who saw them. Close by. Below.

On Christmas

For those who come to this season by no
bright light, it can be so hard to feel joy.

Many have hurt. A night of despair—
divorce or loss of a friend yesterday.

Cost of cancer suffering. Say a dying
child. So they may desire to end. Yet

see the art of van Gogh, his canvas, his heart.
Or Emily Dickinson's pain and poems. She'd dart

too from belief, or parties. Just so: this show
is created for fearful folks to come through

wounds and, like these artists, not always lose
love, beauty, celebration. Many yearly strain

to create, to sculpt and chisel Christmas.
Though love and joy is not all we know,

see and taste. Let it glow.

Memory

for Kathryn Moody: Maw

Petals. Two ebbed peonies
Wane from stems to the table:

Pink. White. Pushy prime past.
Their drying tinges are like

Us when we were together.
Smelly with yesterday's fresh

Newness, now deepening. What
Stays? Nothing. Not even this

Spring will last.

Dickinson's Black Lace

All day cold rain betrays the yellow buds.
They leave the sun. They face this lingering gray.

February 2's too dark today for shadows groundhogs
find in fog. And you and she? Your letter came

today, filled yet chilled as February's first
dank Monday. Though she heats that house, it has

no spunk. No spark or wink. It thirsts for spring.
Feels double-crossed. She's here—quite dry

but sunk. She's framed for six more winter weeks
in this bright red brick you said you liked, no,

loved (her place, trimmed white). She fights her bleak
life at this lightless glass. Black loss makes lace.

Advice on Their Ghosts

Some will say they were Madame Bovarys.
Leave their specters alone to dissolve
into myth and die. Some will say
their ashes are history. Some will say
they did not exist except in their minds.

When you met them, they were young,
nearly virginal—even though their bodies
had just given birth. Perhaps they were
Marys of Guadalupe on their way back
to earth by miracle or mistake. They could

have been some sisters you never had.
Maybe just the fallen woman at Jesus'
well. They'll say nail all coffin lids
on their old, old ghosts or echo for you
to hack them to pieces if you dare to muse.

Some will say marry them. They can never
tell you just what to do. You'll see they are
sitting on your shoulder. They'll be touching
your hand, sometimes, and grateful
for memory as you drive an old car

or truck, remember Texas, the sunset.
Their haunts might hail you as your daughters
and sons go, as you laugh, quit your pipe,
become unselfish, or handle your death.
They are dust of you, dear as your soul is.

How could they just disappear?

How You Are Like the House

for Ted

It's a small house. In winter cold leaks through.
The bathroom floor's slanted. Only a tub
four kids scrubbed in. No shower. Grandpa
lived in little attic. Mother and son divided

the large deck into two small ones to make
room for her garden. The living room has
a torn screen door. Only old wall heaters
to warm Texas January cold. Bugs crawl

through the torn window-screens in the heat.
It's sticky Houston. I've known it for years.
I've seen it tens of times: our friends' house, left
to two now by their scattered brood. The mood

I enter when I go there is wonder—something
I cannot explain. That plain house has never
been, for me, twice the same. They may
shuffle a few pieces of furniture they own.

Sometimes the table is cluttered with books.
Or it may be waiting, set for a gourmet meal.
The porch door may be open, or may not.
In winter the house is frigid, in summer hot.

Sometimes rays of yellow afternoon's late light
change everything. Then this house teaches
me a slight, new slant. But the point of this
is not the house—it is how you are like it:

much older than that house is for me—
over forty years—so familiar. Not outdated,
though vintage. Continually turning. I may
have never seen or known the house twice

the same. Broody with tiny surprises, it is
to me as you have been: continually new.

The Wide Net

short story by Eudora Welty

The at first tiny tale: she intends to drown
herself, since (she, pregnant three months)
he "stepped out" on her—just one night.

The expanding rooms of Mississippi story:
His pal says, "It ain't like Hazel." "No," he says,
"Not 't'all. She's terrible feared of water.

How'd she done it?" "Easy. Jumped off back'ards."
And they fetch the very wide net to seine
the infinite river. Hazel, so angry,

simply crouches behind the small stove in her
kitchen. Yet the net, oh yes, that shoreless net . . .
sweeps far and wide and knits the whole town

tightly together, and the county too. Rich,
poor, black white—in true community.
Poor Hazel becomes the huge Holy Grail,

and before he (afterwards) wants to assail
her in desire over his knee—and she, giggling,
won't have it, their affection has connected

everything. "She was just waitin' her chance"
for revenge, his friend means. But the spacious
gods were waiting their own opportunity too,

as they do, to use the blanketing
net for their use. *Isn't it sort of like*
us—not us like him or Hazel, but those

out in the county yearning to be caught?
Isn't it what all our hype about
"net-works" is? Isn't it like love?

Clear Cut and Burn

I am out here where trees had been rooted.
I am out here where black, death-smoke chokes.

I oversee slash gone—now roots harshly
charred. I think of how hard it was for this

scarred trash to have grown. I see the distance
between our green lives and what's seared to sad

ashes. The feared divorce. Dark funeral pyre.
Habitat bereft of most life. Scorched branches

wasted. Some way we'll grow pine seedlings
in rows here. But someday some wise one may

come to say, "In harvest, or love, over-kill does
not pay." It's not acceptable ecology—

even if cash is high. They'll advise, "Souls sold
are wrong." Will we see the green memory-shrub

that lived to stay? Little growing twigs? They yearned
to remain. Or will we just pass, rushing? On our way

to one more race, as usual, moving on. What
golden trash will we ignite next with deadly match?

Scars

Some second sister and her cancer death:
age twenty-nine. His first wife—Elaine.
The tricks of love are often like the pain
of somebody's son from his first breath

seeming not to love her, throwing a stick
at Mom. He was two. Everyone is lame
from the pain of past. Hates it, will kick
against its pricks. We all know the same

limp near the door of more and more sin,
loathe our Fibber and Molly Magee den
stacked with lead-like stuff. Not enough
time or will to clean. Not unrelated, rough-

ly similar: Think of how at any new dawn
morning glories open and then they yawn,
as if throats could drink truth, beauty all
twenty-four hours. But we see how tall

and tight they shut in bowers each night,
sleep, wait, gain strength to greet great sun
again just once more. Will they grin again?
Like us, they know: each glow of bright

white light is still so terror-filled, stark,
it first thrills, then delves down to dark.

Every Sorrow Can Be Borne

(For Laura Guidry, Lois Stark, Becky Millikin,
Joan Alexander, Carolyn Clemson★)

she said, "if you put it into a tale." At last,
all of Africa was loss for Dinesen: by fire,

a business woe, a marriage-mate, her title,
then her health, her best bond crashed.

Lost lions. Airy continent. Finally, a race.
The worst pain was to face a waste of passion.

Wandering in us all a thousand sagas say, "Tell."
Someone's history: her husband, or son. Budding

young beginnings did not stay. How he is
for her today as Africa was for Karen. Cut off.

Absence is that steeped, deep sadness stories
keep. Ties, like scars, don't heal. Yet are not lost.

★*All friends who lost sons in their twenties.*

Search for Perfect Blue

Each day Lady Helena sought
pure color she claimed she knew
before her world was caught
in less than primary hue.

Her desire was for perfect blue
she thought her lover had. He slips
to the hard edge of their globe. True
to him still, she feels his far, soft lips

touch, draws him to her like the grip
of the pulled tides and the moon.
He lodges there—complete. Could she rip
this container? She sees him. So soon

nothing clear lasts of her hopeful start.
Yet one blue jar still eats her red heart.

In Passing

How many before you have decorated
your house, or died here before you?

How many have loved this past or have
loathed their histories here? Who has

rested her body from a day's tedium?
Who has cooked here for cousins? For

farmers, perhaps, or MD's? Who made
her own bedspread here, taking five

years? Who quilted, neighbors always
helping her, in her front room? Who

took a photograph of whom? Assume
the house has outlasted weather, tornado,

wind and fire. The persons who harbored
here passed first. But what will our kids

do with these buildings? Inherit? Inhabit?
Sell? Well, they could live on or re-invest

house-cash. They could lose it. Use it
or trash. This home you love, the place

you reared them, will pass on. The deed.
So all of you doings. (Including your books.)

They may all pass to strangers. Even
your enemy could end up owning your

locks. Strange knobs and walls. Stranger
keys. Look at our snap-your-finger days

here. Think of them as your ways. Think
these thoughts often, of houses, in passing.

Festina Lente

(honoring Mary Eileen Dobson)

Sarah's God is like a mule working slow plow
Through dirt, while she holds right to the old,
Cracked, oak handle. She has seen many mules till.
She's heard relatives' tales of their plowing cotton

Or corn. Sarah supposes the soil is her life—
Blemish and blight without water
Or fire or air. She and God inch along,
Stop to wipe sweat. They harrow field-ground

Left. *Festina lente*: to make haste
Slowly, with no motor or rush. Speedless,
She and the dumb, neutered animal keep
To their furrow. We can imagine them

Held, harnessed, and freed.

As They Lower My Last Uncle

for Cheryl, Rachel and Jewel Pittman

It's good the light shines here. No darkness, now
in the white cells that took him. Or in the breath

of God on the tape as I play alleluias in a requiem.
I light four fires. Five hundred miles away in cold

January, now they drive several cars to the place
they will lower him into an icy grave. One fire

for his brother, my father, who died thirty-three years
ago, young. Two for their parents. They are all

there fairly close in red clay. Today I say that his
daughter, my sister, and I are all the descendants

not deceased. No male, except I gave my son their
name in his long one, some of their genes. The mass

now is finished, like their lives. Here on this table
before me in light streaming through, near noon,

by three large-paned windows, four fires blaze.
Blue, candled in January sun.

Sybil Pittman Estess was born and reared in Mississippi, took a B.A. at Baylor University, an M.A. at University of Kentucky, and Ph.D. from Syracuse University. She lives in Houston and has taught literature and writing at colleges and universities there and in surrounding towns. She has published poems in many magazines and journals, as well as reviews, critical essays, interviews, a collection of critical essays, and a creative writing text. She has written on Wallace Stevens, Elizabeth Bishop, Denise Levertov, Maxine Kumin and other poets. Sybil is married to Ted L. Estess and is the mother of one son, Barrett.

CPSIA information can be obtained at www.ICGtesting.com
Printed in the USA
BVOW042224120812

297623BV00001B/28/A